7 Steps to Recession-Proofing Your Business

Leverage Your Business for Long-Term Success

Frank Demming

Edited by Deborah Kevin

Copyright © 2017 Frank Demming

All rights reserved.

ISBN-10: 1547245085

ISBN-13: 978-1547245086

DEDICATION

This book is dedicated to my father, Julian R. Demming Sr., and my beautiful wife Rachel.

CONTENTS

	Acknowledgments	i
1	Introduction	1
2	Passion	5
3	Brand	9
4	The Lead Generating Website	11
5	The "No-Brainer" Offer	15
6	The Stair Step Sales Funnel	17
7	The Fortune is in the Follow-Up	19
8	The 4Rs of Marketing	21
9	Next Steps	36
10	Resources	38

ACKNOWLEDGMENTS

My father, Julian R Demming Sr., who is no longer with us, and my beautiful wife Rachel made this book possible.

My father was my hero and my biggest advocate. As I was writing this book, I have had many flash backs of him looking at me and giving me a smile with a look of pride on his face. He sacrificed a lot to give us the best life possible, and the reason I am even able to write this book is because of his sacrifices.

My wife has been my biggest cheerleader these past years. She has believed in me and has accepted my passion to help small business owners throughout the globe, increase their revenue and truly become recession proof. This book is a result of her constant reminder of our purpose in this life.

Frank Demming

1 INTRODUCTION

You're a business owner, most likely a successful one. If you're like many business owners, you experience ebbs and flows in your work — and your income. It's challenging to manage employees or pay expenses (or yourself) when you have so many ups and downs. That's why your investment in this book, which is for **business owners looking to increase their revenues in a relatively short period,** was one of the smartest moves you've ever made.

In this economy, a lot of small or mid-sized business owners struggle to keep their businesses open. They struggle to get a consistent flow of new customers — and keep those they have. You may fit into one (or more) of these scenarios:

- You've been feeling a lull in your business sales, and you're looking for a better strategy;
- You have a website, but it's not a money generating website;
- Networking events are not providing the results quick enough;
- You're not receiving the referrals you expected from Angie's list, Home Advisor, or from purchased leads;
- You want to attract more leads at a lower cost; or
- You're ready to up-level your business and exponentially grow your net worth.

This list could go on indefinitely, but you're a quick study, so you get the point. In preparing to write this book, I researched to determine if other business owners also had similar issues to those I experienced. What I uncovered AMAZED me. Some companies were flush — with clients and with cash. They had what I wanted. I investigated what exactly set those businesses apart from their struggling counterparts. Why did Company "A" struggle to get customers, while Company "B" had plenty of new projects every month?

- Was it because Company B had a better rating on Angie's list or Home Advisor?
- Was it their BBB rating?
- Was it Luck?

The correct answer was "None of the above."

In fact, the answer was simple. Company "B" used the **7-Step Recession-Proofing Your Business Process** which you're about to see, a process that works *regardless of the economy or the industry.*

I created the **7-Step Recession-Proofing Your Business Process** first to impact my own business. It worked. So I shared the plan with other small business owners, who were in a variety of different sales and service-based industries. Guess what? **The blueprint worked for them, too** — regardless of their industry. My clients are now consistently bringing new clients on board, week in and week out.

The **7-Step Recession-Proofing Your Business Process** has worked in industries like:

- Porta-Potty Businesses
- Basement Waterproofing Businesses
- Nursing Schools
- English as a Second Language (ESL) Schools
- Home Remodeling Businesses
- Many others!

Pretty interesting, right? Most importantly, I realized that what I'd discovered was no fluke.

All you have to do is open your local newspaper to the finance section to read about our terrible economy. Maybe you feel fear when you read dire financial outlooks. Here's the thing: every business which has been exposed to my **7-Step Recession-Proofing Your Business Process** is gainfully busy with **new customers every single month**. They're laughing at their competition.

You may be thinking that this sounds too good to be true. I don't blame you. I had similar thoughts before applying the process to my own business.

The truth is that this process has helped DOZENS of small-to-mid-sized business owners across multiple industries, which is why I believe it will also help you. (Which, after all, is the whole reason you've read this far!)

You are about to discover simple steps for how to:

- Quickly and significantly increase your customer base and revenue;
- Strategically grow your net worth;
- Increase the lifetime value for your customers;
- Put your website on the payroll and have it do most of the work for you; and
- Make your competition non-existent.

Plus, if you implement the steps correctly, you will begin to reap the positive effects quickly!

I don't want to mislead you. This process, although simple, will take regular ACTION on your part. As one of my mentors says, "Pray, but move your feet."

Within these pages, you'll find out how to **generate a flood of new and returning customers** in any economy— while your competitors wonder how you're doing it.

Here is the **7-Steps to the Recession-Proofing Your Business Process**:

1. Passion
2. Build Your Brand
3. Your Lead Generating Website
4. The "No-Brainer" Offer
5. The Stair-Step Sales Funnel

6. Fortune is in the Follow-Up
7. The 4 Rs of Marketing

Take action TODAY to begin seeing results in your bottom line right away! I'm invested in you, so please send me your personal success story after you've implemented the 7-Step Recession-Proofing Process. My contact information can be found at the end of this book.

Let's get started!

2 PASSION

Have you ever had a task that you *had* to do, not that you wanted to do? One of mine "have tos" is folding laundry, specifically socks (where does that odd sock wander off to, anyway?).

If you're anything like me, you will do anything to avoid doing those *un-fun* things you *have* to do. On the other hand, when my wife schedules a fun family outing, and I'm suddenly full of energy and excitement. My heart races and I move my entire schedule around to accommodate this outing.

Simply put: you must have the "fun family outing" passion for your business because this level of love keeps you from bailing when the hard times hit. Because they're going to hit. Maybe they already have.

This may sound simple and possibly a little goofy, but it is perhaps **the most important step in this whole process**. If you're not passionate about truly making a difference in your customers' lives, then you might as well close up shop and try something else.

This first step has a lot to do with mindset, and it is a key ingredient to how you approach your business. While the other steps in this process are more tactical, this one is centered and based on **your inner being** and has everything to do with why you are in business in the first place.

I realized that one thing separates the successful business owners from everyone else: they do the things others don't.

You must work harder on yourself than you do on your business — which means **you'll go to the next level every time**.

The opposite is true, too. The moment that your business becomes more important than you, your health, your family, and other commitments, the moment you let yourself get wrapped around all that stuff that comes with owning a business, **you lose your edge, and you lose the thing that makes you irresistible to your customers**.

Don't let that happen to you. (Don't worry, if you already have, we'll do triage to get you back on the right path.) **This one step is what separates you from your competition**. It's what will determine how you attract your ideal customers.

Think about your level of passion. Is it *"have to"* passion or *"I can't believe I get to do this for a living"* passion? If it's the former, what needs to happen to shift it to the latter? Don't lose that lovin' feeling!

Once you're passionately driven again, it's time to develop your Unique Selling Proposition (USP). Already have one? This step will help you refine it so that you are more irresistible.

Developing your USP allows you to grow your business while shifting from *working in* it to *working on* it.

Are you scratching your head, asking, **"What's the difference between working on and working in a business?"** That's okay! *Working in* your business means you aren't effectively delegating tasks to others so that you're burning the midnight oil to get payroll run, taxes filed, proposals written, and other back office tasks that you don't get to during working hours. *Working on* your business keeps you focused on strategic growth, leveraging your processes, and has you fulfilling a managerial role.

Working in your business will hurt your profits and doesn't necessarily mean you have a true passion for the business.

And we can't have that — especially because we want to recession-proof your business. That being said, here are a few pointers for developing your USP. In a nutshell, the secret to coming up with a USP that separates you from your competitors is how well you can tap into your customer's subconscious mind. The foundation for your USP must come from a real understanding of your customer. Here are a few ways you develop that understanding:

- **Think like your customer.** Step outside of your day-to-day role of owner and think about what your customers want from your service. What is it that makes them come back again and again, instead of going to your competition? It might be the quality or convenience. Perhaps it is your friendliness, exceptional customer service, or reliability. Remember that people do not do business with you solely for price alone. Hopefully, there are qualities that attract and appeal to your customer base.
- **Learn what motivates your customer's buying decisions.** You need to know what drives and motivates your customers. Having some knowledge of your target market's demographics is essential, but, just as importantly, you must learn how they derive gratification in life and what their purchase preferences are. People buy products and services primarily based on their desires, not on their needs. Knowing these desires and motivations will help inform your true unique selling proposition.
- **Know the real reasons customers come to you instead of your competition.** How do you do that? Ask your customers. This can be done in a wide variety of ways from face-to-face conversations to surveys to focus groups. Every business lends itself to certain methods of deriving this information, but the fundamental truth is that you can never know too much about your customers!
- **Determine what features of your business stand out as something that sets you apart from the pack.** What can you highlight that will move prospective customers to do business with you? And how can you position everything you do in your business to embody that USP?

Once you have completed the basic understanding of your customer's desires, you must now bring your USP to life. Start out by asking yourself, what should an effective USP look like? I know that is a difficult question to answer, so I'm going to simplify it for you. The real power of your USP comes from its connection to the unconscious mind. Once you have dedicated some careful thought to understanding the collective minds of your target market, you can then concentrate that understanding into how you need to position your business. The way to craft a powerful USP is to make sure it ties into the most emotionally stimulating elements of your customers' experience with your business. So how do you capture this in a short phrase that touches on emotional gratification promised by your service? Follow these seven simple yet powerful guidelines:

1. Make the phrase short. In other words, make it a phrase, and not a sentence;
2. Keep it vague enough to leave room for the imagination of your reader;
3. Convey a positive feeling;
4. Give it impact and emotion;
5. Avoid defining your business as a commodity;
6. Focus on the promise of emotional gratification – the result or benefit – not the work or features you offer; and
7. Make it consistent with the general perception of your business and what you have learned of your customer's gratification mode and purchase preferences.

One last tip on this, don't feel that you have to be "married" to your USP. It is my experience that successful businesses often develop new USPs as they grow and evolve. And the more you learn about your customers and what constitutes your promise of emotional gratification, the clearer your understanding of what an effective Unique Selling Proposition will be. Ultimately, the real acid test is to ask yourself, "What emotion am I selling?"

3 BRAND

Every business ought to have a well-defined brand. If you've been in business for a while, you may say to yourself, "I have a brand." That may be true, but you may not be utilizing your brand effectively.

What exactly is a brand? In the purest sense of the word, a brand is a promise. Think about Apple. Their promise is to be cutting edge rebels who deliver kung-fu, kick-like power. Volvo, by contrast, is known for safety.

Another definition is that a brand is a combination of font, color, and image to create a unique look that is, hopefully, instantly recognizable. Brands like Kodak, Coca-Cola, Ford, and McDonald's are universally recognizable no matter where you happen to see them.

Investing in a brand is worthwhile. In developing your brand, the last thing you want to do is copycat what's already been done. Your brand needs to capture your USP and plant itself in the hearts and minds — especially hearts — of your ideal clients.

The best brands are memorable. Yours ought to be, too, because it will be the focus of all your marketing efforts. Your brand needs to say a lot: about your company, your target market, and motivate your clients in a way that creates loyalty.

Successful local businesses like Johnson's Landscaping, DWM Roofing Inc., RotoRooter, and Big Dog Remodelers Inc., have seen the positive effect that branding has on franchise businesses and have modeled it for their benefit.

Here's an interesting factoid: **93%** of all franchise businesses are successful. Why? Because the brand is already recognized and developed. Think about it. When was the last time McDonald's changed their logo? And I'm sure every time you hear the words, "A little dab'll do ya" you automatically associate it with Brylcreem (now I'm showing my age!).

The point is branding works, and it is VITAL for your business to stand a chance in today's business environment. The best form of branding is to ensure that your **logo incorporates an effective tagline with it**. Try to tie the slogan to what your USP is.

You want your prospects to see your logo with your tagline and recognize your company. This is important because, once they are ready, your company will be the first ones they call. It's called being "top of mind."

Back in the day, grabbing potential customers' attention was done via billboards and advertisements. Today, the same outreach is more effective using social media and remarketing, which will put your branding practices on steroids. [What's remarketing? Remarketing is a way to connect your website with visitors who may not have made an immediate purchase or inquiry. It allows you to position targeted ads in front of a defined audience that previously visited your website — as they browse elsewhere around the internet. Facebook users are quite familiar with this practice.]

Branding is a huge component to your success and establishing one that becomes a part of your customers' lives is crucial because it will keep them away from your competitors. That being said, I'd like to give you six crucial branding practices to ensure that your business is truly recession proof.

1. **When building your brand, think of it as a person.** Every one of us is an individual whose character is made up of beliefs, values, and purposes that define who we are and who we connect with. Our personality determines how we behave in different situations, how we dress, and what we say. Of course, for people it's intuitive, and it's rare that you even consider what your character is, but when you're building a brand, it's vital to have that understanding.

2. **Consider what is driving your business.** What does it believe in, what is its purpose and who are its brand heroes? These things can help establish your brand positioning and

inform the identity and character for brand communications.

3. **Aim to build long-term relationships with your customers.** Don't dress up your offering and raise expectations that result in broken promises, create trust with honest branding — be clear who your company is and be true to the values that drive it every day.

4. **Speak to your customers with a consistent tone of voice.** It will help reinforce the business' character and clarify its offering, so customers are aware exactly what to expect from your service.

5. **Don't mimic the look of chains or big brands.** Try and carve out your distinctive identity. There is a consumer trend towards independent establishments, and several chains are trying to mimic an independent feel to capture some of that market. Truly independent operators can leverage their status to attract customers who are looking for something more original and authentic that aligns with how they feel about themselves.

6. **Be innovative, bold and daring. Stand for something you believe in.** Big brands are encumbered by large layers of bureaucracy, preventing them from being flexible and reacting to their customers' ever-changing needs. Those layers of decision-makers can make it hard for them to be daring with their branding.

4 THE LEAD GENERATING WEBSITE

Does your company have a website? Is it an active part of your marketing or is it a static place for clients to find you on the web?

I ask these questions because many companies already have a website and many are already using their websites as a signature or a branding piece of their business. However, the sites are not optimized for success.

Having a website is great, but if the only way your customers can communicate with you is for them to pick up the phone and call you, you're leaving about **90% of your revenue potential** on the table.

That's right. **90% of your potential revenue**.

When people search the internet for a product or a service, they aren't always ready to take action. Likely, they're simply researching possibilities. They're checking reviews. Making mental lists.

But if your website provided an avenue for you to collect your potential clients' names and email addresses, you would have an opportunity to convert them into customers later when they are ready. Having their contact information allows you to woo them, thus keeping your business 'top of mind.'

> **Ninja Hint**: Keeping your information in front of your potential customers will also keep them further away from your competition.

Let's have some fun with numbers. If you get 1,000 visitors to your website on a daily basis, but you aren't positioned to capture the lead properly (i.e., using a capture form, offering a newsletter, or having a chat session in place), you miss the opportunity to develop a relationship with your lead. At 1,000 visitors a day, you're losing potentially 365,000 potential leads. Why have a website at all?

Ensure your website is structured in a way that helps you capture your visitors. Put that site to work and make it earn its pay! Doing so brings you one step closer to generating the revenue you are looking for.

Now let's talk about some website fundamentals. I recommend hiring a professional design company to design and build your website. Not only that, I'd say make sure that the company your hire specializes in websites for small businesses. Gone are the days when you can get your "cousin's friend John" to design your website. Although he may be technically proficient, and produce a very elegant and professional looking website, he probably isn't savvy enough to know what is the best methodology to use to ensure your website generates business.

Another tip is to ensure that your website is mobile responsive. This may seem obvious, and it has become pretty common (especially since Google has made it a mandatory practice towards the end of 2015); however, I recently found several websites that were not mobile responsive, and it totally shocked me. Don't overlook this key aspect.

Perhaps the most important aspects of your website are the content and messaging. And here is where a professional can help you convert 40 – 50% of your website visitors into real leads. Earlier we talked about having several ways for your website to capture the visitor's information. The messaging on your website is what guides them into taking action. Your website must create an emotional response for your visitors. When you understand who your ideal client is, and build your content around that understanding (make sure you do the exercise on Chapter 1), you will build rapport with your visitors, tug on their emotional needs, and convert them into leads.

Your website ought to be the cornerstone of your marketing plan. That's why you must ensure that it is designed to build your pipeline and position you in a way that it eliminates any competition. When your business resonates with your visitors before they've picked up the phone and called, or filled out the form to inquire more, you are guaranteed to generate loyal fans of your business/brand for years to come.

5 THE "NO-BRAINER" OFFER

In the last chapter, we asked if your website was doing the heavy lifting. In this chapter, we'll show you one way to make it work for you. We're going tactical! These days, you have to be willing to give something to get something. And what you want is your potential clients' contact information.

Let's say you have a construction business and you specialize in remodeling kitchens. You could put an offer on your website which would give new clients a few free appliances for their kitchen. Not only would this be easy to arrange but, more importantly, it separates you from your competition, and make the decision for your customer a "no-brainer."

Here's another example: One of my clients owns a Peruvian restaurant in the Washington, D.C. area. He struggled to land new customers because there were so many restaurant choices for diners to choose from in his particular neighborhood. Frankly, there wasn't anything "special" about his place. We audited his website, consulted with him for about an hour or so, and suggested that he create the following "no-brainer" offer and place it on his website: *"Receive $20 worth of food for $10."*

Here's what happened: He is now a **very** popular restaurant on that strip. Each and every day his restaurant is packed with new customers, wanting to take advantage of that sweet deal.

More importantly, he is now getting **repeat** customers. By making a "no-brainer" offer, he expanded his reach into the neighborhood. Because his food and service are excellent, repeat business is a given.

What kinds of "no-brainer" offers could you make to attract your idea clients?

Here are a few examples of some "no-brainer" offers I have helped some of my customers develop.

- **Chiropractors**: you can create a "no-brainer" offer of a free massage. To accomplish this, develop an alliance with a massage therapist. Once set up, you are all but guaranteed to receive a flood of leads into your practice.
- **Personal Injury Lawyers**: one of the things you can have a running offer on your website, where every last Thursday of each month, you hold a free talk on advice concerning personal injury topics. Pick a topic of the month and you will generate plenty of interested guests on a monthly basis. People LOVE free advice from a reputable lawyer.
- **Dentists:** a common "no-brainer" offer is free teeth cleaning. So, let me give you another idea that will set you apart from your competitors. Offer your first-time customers a credit towards any service you offer. I'd say you place this offer on your signature service (cosmetic dentistry, root canal, braces, composite fillings, etc.). The credit can be a dollar amount or a percentage. I've seen it work well either way.

These are just a few examples of a few industries. There a dozens of "no-brainer" offers you can develop. A good tip for developing your "no-brainer" is to ensure that it is tied to your USP and that it accentuates your brand. Make sure that you work with a small business marketing consultant to ensure that you develop the right "no-brainer" best suited for your business and your audience.

Having a "no-brainer" offer to attract leads is a good thing, however, if you do not have a process in place to convert those leads into actual paying customers, then you have lost the battle.

The next chapter will ensure that you win the battle and that you gain repeat customers as well.

6 THE STAIR STEP SALES FUNNEL

What would happen to your cash flow or your bottom line if you increased the lifetime value of your customer by **20%**? How about increasing the value by **40%**?

The definition of a sales funnel (also known as a revenue funnel or sales process) is the buying process that companies lead customers through when purchasing products or services. A sales funnel is divided into several steps, which differ depending on the particular sales model.

Here is where you will start to realize the value of every one of your customers. This "*stair-step sales funnel*" will keep your customers happy and will keep you in business for a LONG time. More importantly, this is where you will undoubtedly increase your revenue and start to build significant net worth.

Let's go back to our kitchen remodeling construction company example. Can we agree that having at least one additional specialty like bathroom or basement remodeling would be a good idea for this company (not to mention a sound business practice)?

While the crew works on the kitchen remodel, the foreman notices that the customer's bathroom could use some upgrading. By making a few simple suggestions about what they could do in their bathroom to bring it up-to-date or more attractive, the foreman could give them a quote, right then and there.

Here's what other business owners in the home services industry have experienced when implementing this tactic: a **new project** was generated with the same customer at least **3 out of 10 times.** A word of caution: the proper approach is crucial. The technique is to have your stair-step sales funnel already in place and know **how best to position it** at the right time.

Here's another real-world example of how this works: A

successful air duct cleaning company in the D.C. area had a "no-brainer" offer for air duct cleaning priced at $49. (If you are unfamiliar with the value of an air duct cleaning, the cost is typically between $200-$400, depending on the size of your home.)

Here is how the air duct company worked their stair-step sales funnel. As they completed the quality air duct cleaning service for a measly $49, they offered their client a maintenance contract for $99/month so the customer would never again worry about polluted or contaminated air circulating through their ducts. Additionally, the company tacked on a maintenance contract for the furnace and air conditioning system for $399/year. Because the client is delighted with the clean air ducts and the quality service provided, they're more likely to sign-up for additional services right then. These value-added services cement the relationship, as well as growing your bottom line.

Are you able to see how this step ties in with having a "no-brainer" offer as well as how powerful the stair-step sales funnel is?

In today's marketplace, the businesses that survive and outperform their competitors, understand how to move their current clientele from one service offering to another, pretty effortlessly. It's simply understanding the core needs of your ideal customers and positioning your marketing and sales process to bring forth the solutions.

This is a key component in having a recession proof business. Having customers is one thing, but having repeat customers puts you on a whole different level. If you feel that your business is a one-time business, I invite you to think again. That does not exist. You need to work with a local business marketing consultant to help you package your offerings and reposition your business in the marketplace showcasing your new brand.

Can you think of different and innovative ways in which this can work for you?

7 THE FORTUNE IS IN THE FOLLOW-UP

Let's face it, competition is fierce out there, and if you're not following up with the people who come in contact with you via your website, they will simply go with your competitor.

Are you following me?

Let's explore this idea further through an example. Let's say you own a construction company, and through effective marketing, a potential client found you via a search engine like Google, Bing, or Yahoo. This potential client wanted a company that could upgrade their kitchen.

Just collecting the name and email address of your lead isn't enough. You need to have a streamlined follow-up system, which will position you and your company as who they want to do business with. In other words, you need to nurture these leads.

If you don't have a follow-up system, they will simply go to your competitor, because it is highly likely that if they found you on the internet, they probably found others as well.

So how do you follow-up? There are several options, but the best one is to *just do it*! You nurture your leads via telephone, email, or in-person. It's also great to utilize all avenues to touch base with these folks.

Whichever way you go with, it is important that you follow-up with your potential customers **within 24 hours** of them visiting your site and soliciting for more information about your services.

The second point is that you need to have at least **eight communication touches** with them within a 12 - 15 day period. These touches can be either via email, the phone, postcard, etc. The key is they need to be concentrated in a period of 12 - 15 days because research shows that having eight touches during a 12 - 15 day period increases your conversion rate by a whopping **425%**.

That's pretty significant, don't you think?

Yes, it is. But I know what you are probably thinking, where are you going to find the time to do all of this follow-up? How are you going to compete with your larger competitors who have the manpower to do all of this follow-up?

No worries, I've got you covered. All you need to do is invest is some marketing automation tools to help you out. You can automate the entire process so all of your follow-ups are done for you.

There are many tools out there for you to choose from. There's Infusionsoft, Ontraport, ActiveDemand, Active Campaign, etc. Now, sometimes, in all honesty, these tools can be rather complicated to configure and map to your businesses processes. However, don't get discouraged. The best way to combat that is to hire a small business marketing consultant and have them build an in-house tool that is aligned well with your current operations and that will build in the follow-up process that you want to instill.

Having fun yet?

8 THE 4RS OF MARKETING

Whether you have a brick and mortar business or strictly an e-Commerce business, you need to generate traffic. More importantly, you want to ensure that a good percentage of that traffic converts into customers. For this step to be effective, you need to make sure that all of the steps above are already in place, **before you start to generate traffic**.

Are we clear on that? Good.

Over the years that I've been in business, I have learned that just getting traffic is not enough. It's vital to have an effective strategy in place to ensure that the traffic flow is solid and well-informed as to what products and services you offer and how they are delivered.

What are the 4 Rs of Marketing?
The 4 R's are:

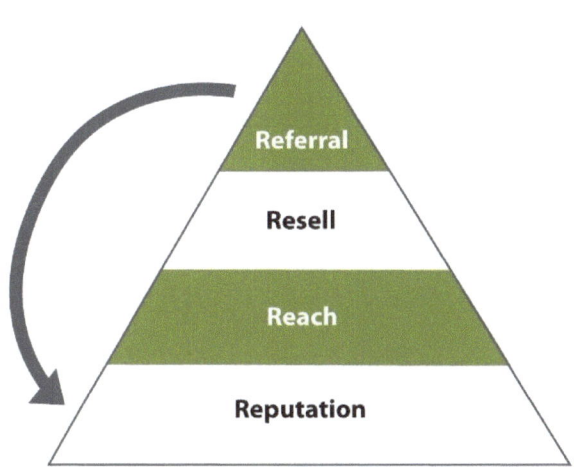

R1 Reputation
R2 Reach
R3 Resell
R4 Referral

These are the four things *every* business needs to plan for and optimize to maximize their growth potential. Data shows and my experience proves that each of these can account for about 25% growth on their own, and combined have a compounding effect that can ignite growth to 100% or more.

R1: Reputation

It has never been easier for potential customers to find out what others think about your business. This is both good and bad (depending on what people find).

__Think__: What are you doing to proactively manage, protect, and monetize your most valuable asset: your reputation?

As you probably know, nowadays people search online before they buy. It's also true that people put a lot of stock in what they find and read online. In fact, a recent Nielsen study shows that 74% of U.S. consumers choose to do business based on online feedback—even when it's feedback from total strangers!

According to Nielsen's summary of their poll data, recommendations from personal acquaintances and opinions posted by consumers online are "the most trusted forms of advertising."

A short list of who is talking about your business, include but is not limited to:

- Customers;
- Prospects;
- Competitors;
- Disgruntled employees;
- Former business partners, investors; and
- Trolls (the permanently aggrieved).

This brings up a larger point – whether positive or negative in tone, most of the content about your business available online is not even being created by you anymore! Consumers are critics and publishers now. They all carry tiny "printing presses" in their pockets!

Businesses have always relied on their reputation, but the stakes are even higher today because of how easy it is for consumers to find information about companies before they buy. What's more, as we've already discussed, negative reviews can get lodged in the search results, hanging like an albatross around your neck and dragging down sales.

***Ask yourself**: Are you "Google-able"? How many pages of Google are you on? (You may include Search, Maps, and Google+ Local citations in your answer)*

- ☐ Don't know
- ☐ 0
- ☐ 1
- ☐ 2–5
- ☐ 6+

R2: Reach

What are you doing to ensure that more people know about you today than they did yesterday? It's my experience that businesses that want to grow need to make sure that more people know more about them each day.

If you're not meeting new people and telling them about your products and services, you're not developing a pipeline of potential new customers, and, as a result, you are going to see fewer sales.

This sounds obvious, but I'm always surprised when I talk to business owners and ask them about their promotional efforts. When I look at the pipeline filling activities of businesses, I see mostly a scattershot approach. That is to say, a campaign here and there, with only a vague idea of whether they are getting a positive return on their investment. It's no wonder so many businesses become skeptical of marketing. They're doing it wrong!

Very rarely do I see coordinated, systematic, and metrics-driven efforts to reach a wider audience and drive more prospects (i.e., people who are interested in what you're selling) through the front door. This kind of focused, ongoing, and intentional approach is exactly what's necessary to reach more qualified prospects in a cost-effective and satisfying manner.

__Ask yourself__: Do you have a consistent method to build a growing prospect/client email list?
- ☐ Yes
- ☐ No
- ☐ I don't have a list

R3: Resell

What are you doing to upsell, cross-sell, and repeat sell to maximize the lifetime value of your customer base? Once you've done all of the hard and often costly work of getting a customer, you need to make sure to maximize the lifetime value (LTV) of that customer.

__Think__: Attracting a new customer can cost five times as much as keeping an existing one (Lee Resource Inc. Study).

It makes more sense (both financially and from an efficiency standpoint) to fully capitalize on your existing customer base, rather than to be constantly on the hunt for new customers. The more value you can generate from each customer, the less you have to spend on marketing, which means you can increase your profit margins and/or reinvest the savings into your products and services—in the process making your business even more attractive to your customers!

In practice, this can mean increasing the dollar value of each transaction or increasing the frequency that customers buy, either by offering add-on services or upsells or cross-sells. McDonald's offers the classic example: "Do you want fries with that?" or "Do you want to supersize your order?"

These days there are so many cost-effective and trackable ways to bring customers back to your business. Here's one example, consider short message service (SMS or text message) coupon campaigns. With monthly costs lower than $30 to send 1,000 text messages and an average redemption rate of 20% or more, this highly successful campaign costs less than 30 cents per customer.

Despite having easy access to new and cool tools, most small businesses leave money on the table because they're not maximizing the resell potential of each customer.

Ask Yourself: *Do you ethically (but effectively) prepare buyers from their very first purchasing experience with you to keep coming back to purchase over and over again?*
- ☐ No
- ☐ Yes
- ☐ Not sure

R4: Referral
What are you doing to use your successful relationships to create new, organic opportunities so that you can spend less and make more? The next best thing you can do for your business is to set up systems to maximize the benefit you get from your customers. To have them advocate for you (e.g., word of mouth), you have to make it very easy—almost effortless—for your happy customers to refer your business to others.

Think: *Customers that come from referrals, on average, are 18% more likely than others to stay with a company and generate 16% more in profits (Harvard Business Review)!*

Referrals make great customers
We all want referrals because they help us save money on marketing, right? Well, there's even more to gain from referrals than cost savings.

According to several case studies reported on by the website TechCrunch, "Friends referred by friends make better customers. They spend more (two times higher estimated lifetime value versus customers); convert better (75% higher conversion than from other marketing channels); and hop faster (they make their first purchase after joining twice as quickly as referrals from other channels)."

Why are referrals so powerful?
Referrals are powerful because they leverage social proof. Social proof is a fancy way of saying that we humans are easily influenced by each other. We're pack animals, and when a member of our pack (family) or tribe (social circle) recommends a product or service, we take that recommendation seriously. Similarly, when someone in a position of power, prestige, or authority recommends something, we are very quick to act on that recommendation.

You witness the applied power of social proof everywhere: in celebrity endorsing TV ads; on the radio, when the person hosting the pledge drive tells listeners that so-and-so donated $50; on the back of a novel you're reading, when you see reviews from other notable authors; and on the web, when you visit sites like Yelp.com to read consumer reviews about local restaurants.

Moving from passive to active, ad hoc to systematic
Almost without fail, most businesses I talk to have no clear referral generation system. They essentially think that referrals are something that you simply wait and hope for, but the reality is that referrals don't just happen, you have to go out and get them! And if you're going to spend the time collecting them, you need a system that effectively channels your efforts into tangible results.

Ask Yourself*: How many formal, written referral generating systems do you currently have with prospects or potential partners?*
- ☐ 0
- ☐ 1
- ☐ 2–5
- ☐ 6+

What are you missing?

Think*: Sixty percent of users will leave a website if it's not optimized for mobile (Google Study).*

The problem is that most businesses are operating without even being aware of these changes or marketing systems, and how it is impacting their business.

If you aren't effectively and proactively managing your reputation, you aren't aware of comments like this being made about your business:

Or, you have people looking for your business on their mobile phones, and your website is showing up like the image below on the left? No one has fingers small enough, or enough patience, to navigate this web page.

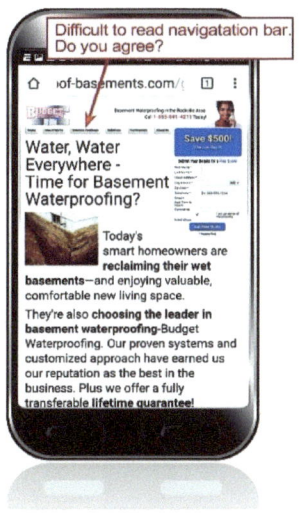 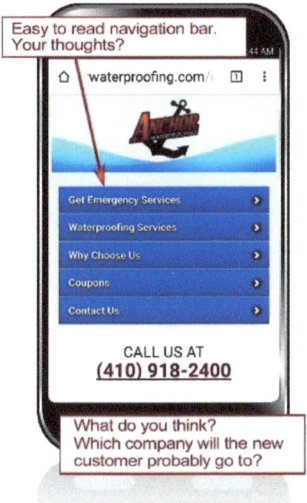

Poorly Designed Mobile Site   **Well Designed Mobile Site**

How can we address some of these issues? Here are a few ideas:

- Control your reviews with your robust review generating process;
- Create a separate site for your business that is

optimized for mobile; and
- Use Facebook ads and Local Search Optimization to reach more people in a cost-effective way and with greater targeting.

Is your business being left behind?

If you fall into the category of businesses that are not proactively working with these technology changes and marketing systems, you are only going to see things get worse over time. These changes, though recent, are now a permanent part of the competitive landscape. The gap between the businesses that "get it" and those that don't is widening at an accelerating pace

You can look at any industry and see examples of the handful of businesses that are pulling away from the pack, and those that are falling behind.

It's time to go 'all in'

Do you have someone who is helping your business in these areas? Or are you kidding yourself into thinking that you are going to try to do this by yourself or with the very part-time effort of one of your employees that have no marketing background?

If you're struggling to fit everything into your calendar already (most business owners I talk to are), you may not have the bandwidth to optimize the four R's. Either something else has to give, or you need to enlist a friendly expert to help you!

Answer the call

Are you ready, both literally and figuratively, to answer that call? Or are you going to let the phone ring until one of your competitors answers the call?

__Think__: Data from Google indicates that 61% of local searches on a mobile phone result in a phone call.

Focusing on the 4 Rs of marketing, let's look at four highly effective ways to generate traffic to your website.

1. **Search Engine Optimization (SEO)**. Get the search engines to LOVE your website. You need to **optimize** your website for a few strategically targeted keyword phrases and ensure that your site will appear on the first page of the search engines when your potential customers type in the keyword phrases you are targeting.

SEO is an extremely effective traffic driving strategy and happens to be the strategy that converts the most visitors into customers, therefore, I wanted to ensure I mentioned it first.

The secret to getting SEO to work for you is to ensure that you find the **right keywords** that your potential customers are typing in their search bars. Make sure that you do extensive research on Google or use a word tracker-based tool to search for the proper keywords. The key to finding the right keyword(s) making sure you find the keywords with a high search volume, but with low competition. This can be tricky, but here's a secret tool you can use that will make this process a lot easier for you. SEOBook (http://www.seobook.com/) will help you determine which keywords are your ideal keywords that will attract your ideal customers.

It's so amazing — and often supplies answers on what your potential clients are searching for, how often per day are they looking. Plus, you'll discover what sort of competition you are going to have in terms of ranking for that keyword quickly.

Once you find at least 20 - 30 highly searched keyword phrases with low competition, you will need to ensure that each of your keywords is in the title tags of your website.

After that, you need is Link Juice, more boringly called backlinks.

2. **Backlinks**. The quickest way to create and utilizes backlinks is to use One Hour Backlinks (http://onehourbacklinks.co/). What is a backlink, you ask? A backlink is an incoming hyperlink from one web page to another website. Getting the right number of backlinks to

your site will put you on top of the search engines within 10 - 15 days of starting the process.

Backlinks can be difficult to understand, and it is difficult for me to teach you the exact science of this traffic method on this book. Selecting and creating effective backlinks are part art and science. You're invited to schedule a call with me to learn more. My contact information can be found at the back of this book.

Before moving on to the next strategy, I just want to talk about a forgotten SEO strategy, blogging. Blogging, when done correctly, can be a powerful tool/strategy to increase search engine traffic to your website(s). Here's why this is so elegant: blogging is considered to be an SEO strategy, so it yields the same conversion ratio, which is what we want. But you need to know how to do it for you the get the right results.

Statistics from Hubspot's 2014 Inbound Marketing Report highlight the importance of blogging. According to the study, 57% of companies who have a blog reported acquiring a customer from their blog. In that same study, a survey of marketers revealed that 81% of businesses say that their business blog is useful to critical for their business.

Here are some of the most important benefits of having a blog for your business:

> A. **Boost Search Engine Optimization**. Search engines love fresh content. What better way to provide frequent content than with blog posts. By blogging consistently, you give Google, and other search engines, new content to index and you create opportunities to plug in those all-important keywords to increase your visibility on search engine results pages (SERPS).
>
> B. **Develop Relationships with Potential and Existing Customers**. Blogging allows you to connect with your site visitors. This can be accomplished by asking

your readers questions at the end of your posts to get the conversation going or by simply allowing comments and feedback. By reviewing and responding to readers' comments, you create a rapport with your audience, build trust, and gain valuable insight into what your customers are looking for.

C. **Establish Your Business as an Industry Leader.** No matter how small your business is, you build trust and clout within your industry by providing valuable, expert information in your blog posts. Over time, you become a "go to" resource for helpful, informative content, which can lead to higher customer conversion rates. This is especially important for small businesses looking to gain credibility to compete with larger companies.

D. **Connect People to Your Brand**. Blog posting allows you to show a personal side of your business that perspective and current customers won't see through outbound marketing techniques. Blogging gives others a sense of the corporate standards, vision, and personality of your company.

E. **Create Opportunities for Sharing.** Every time you publish a blog post, you create an opportunity for your audience to share your blog with others. Whether they link to your blog post, tweet it, or email it to others, it's free marketing, and it further validates you as a credible business.

3. **Social media.** (Facebook, Twitter, LinkedIn, Google +, etc.) Social media is here to stay, and it is today's version of word of mouth marketing. Let's take a look at Facebook alone for a moment.

We've all heard enough hype about social media to last a lifetime.

So many people's perspective on Facebook is based on how they've seen their kids use it. It's a common misconception that Facebook is just for kids. But many wonder: how on earth can Facebook be used for business? In analyzing how social media can impact a company's bottom line, it is critical for business owners to know some relevant statistics and facts:

- In the U.S., almost two-thirds of all Facebook users are *over* the age of 35.

- Over 1.94 billion active users worldwide are on Facebook, 80% of which access through their mobile device. These eyeballs can be monetized!

- Facebook users aren't just ON the site; they're GLUED to it! On average, these users check their newsfeed from their phone app *14 times per day*!

While these users are primarily using Facebook to engage with their friends and family, they are all potential customers. Whether a business is B2B or B2C, the ads component on Facebook is an exceptional option for businesses! There's no other platform where small businesses can reach a granular, targeted audience for their products or services — right down to specific demographics, such as zip code, age, income level, and even the likelihood of making certain purchases. By effectively putting Facebook to work in this manner, small businesses can reach their target customers with laser-like precision. The ROI for business owners through this method is tremendous!

Having a proactive online social media presence that is focused on the appropriate demographics, and which contains *good content*, is the surest way for a small business to reach their target audience. For most businesses, if you don't have a presence on Facebook, you don't even exist! Nowadays, the same is true for small businesses. Whatever niche a small business has, they have to realize they can use social media to be known as "THE GO TO EXPERT" for when a prospective customer has a need for their product or service. No doubt about it, business owners need to capture the attention of their target customers, in a fun, relevant way, or else their competitors will.

You must have a social media presence and strategically share information about your services throughout the social networks. When done correctly and in conjunction with the SEO strategy, your business will skyrocket because your website will constantly be **positioned in front of all your target market**.

The "major" secret behind a successful social media campaign is to create a business page on Facebook or Google + (for example) and have frequent updates and conversations about your products and services within the page. Make sure that your followers are always kept abreast of what you have going on in your company.

But how do you get followers? Good question.

You simply add your current customers to your Facebook or Google + page and create a buzz there. Then you will get into the warm market of your current customers and grow new potential customers from that.

Pretty slick, right?

Yes, it is, and the beauty is that it's free advertising. Just spend the time doing these little key things, and you'll have a GREAT word of mouth marketing strategy working on autopilot.

You may be thinking to yourself, "Wow, that's pretty time consuming."

The truth is it could be. However, with the proper guidance, you'll see that this strategy will only set you back up to 30 mins a day, perhaps less. If you don't have 30 mins to spare, the good news is you can outsource it and just reap the benefits of its outcome.

Is all of this coming together for you?

4. **Mobile Marketing.** Unless you have been under a rock or something for the past few years, you probably have noticed

that mobile devices are a major part of our lives now. Seemingly, everyone has a Smartphone or a tablet, which means HUGE marketing exposure for you. According to research from Mobile Marketer, 70% of all mobile searches result in action within one hour. All you need to do is get yourself a mobile-ready website and position your website on one of the various mobile marketing networks (make sure that you specify what industry you are in and your target market) and your business (products or services) will be in your potential customers' faces at all times.

A recent article in the Economist adds this, "The potential of the smartphone age is deceptive. We look around and see more people talking on the phones in more places and playing Draw Something when they're bored. This is just the beginning. In time, business models, infrastructure, legal environments, and social norms will evolve, and the world will become a very different and dramatically more productive place."

In other words, wherever your potential customers are, **your products and services will be with them as well**, because they will likely have their mobile device with them. Just ensure you select the proper mobile network and strategy to ensure maximum exposure.

One of the best networks to use is admob (https://www.google.com/admob/), but there are others out there that come highly recommended as well. One of these is Geo-Fencing. Geo-Fencing has the capability to identify a target area and show your ad(s) to your potential customers. Let me give you an example so that you know just how powerful this is. Let's assume you are a Honda dealership and you want to target anyone who enters a rivaling Toyota dealership. We can place a "Geo-Fence" around that dealership and have Honda ads show up on the phone of any consumer who entered that particular Toyota's dealership.

Oh, it even gets more interesting than that. You can Geo-Fence only the people who enter the dealership showroom. In other words, if regular Toyota consumers enter the service area because they need to get their car serviced, they won't see the Honda ads. Only people who enter the Toyota showroom will see your ad because the assumption is made that they are in the market for a new car.

Isn't that fascinating? Think of how something that powerful could help build and exponentially grow your business. Think about how you can begin to distance yourself from your competitors. Mobile marketing changes the game so start seriously thinking about implementing these tactics to recession-proof your business.

There are more traffic generating methods, however, following these three ways of generating traffic along with setting up the other steps of this amazing process, will ensure that you get potential customers coming to your **website each and every day for years to come**.

Can you see the power of this remarkable **7-Step Recession-Proofing Your Business Process**?

I sincerely hope that you found this information useful. My first and primary focus has been and continues to be, helping you use your website appropriately so that you can **maximize your profits**.

For me, the payoff is when I get an email or phone call to let me know that you have seen a significant increase in revenue after successfully applying these simple strategies. That is truly rewarding …and happens to be what keeps me going.

9 NEXT STEPS

Congratulations! You made it to the end of this book, which is just the beginning of your implementation process. This book contained a lot of juicy details, right? Don't let yourself feel overwhelmed. These steps are simple, but they are not easy. I know by implementing the **7-Step Recession-Proofing Process,** you will transform your business.

Let's review the **7-Steps to Recession-Proofing Your Business Process**:

1. Passion: Be in love with your business. Create a compelling USP;
2. Build Your Brand: Your brand speaks for you when you aren't around;
3. Your Lead Generating Website: Proven methods to capture and convert leads;
4. The "No-Brainer" Offer: Create something of value to your ideal customers;
5. The Stair-Step Sales Funnel: Have a process in place for what comes next;
6. Fortune is in the Follow-Up: Implement a regular stay-in-touch campaign; and
7. The 4 Rs of Marketing: Reputation, Reach, Resell, and Referral.

You have to take action TODAY to begin seeing results in your bottom line right away! I'm invested in you, so please send me your personal success story after you've implemented the **7-Step Recession-Proofing Process.**

Your business transformation is only beginning. You must **position yourself correctly,** from a marketing standpoint, so that you **TRULY** standout from your competition. Invest in a **professional analysis** on your current website (if you have one) and your marketing practices. Identifying gaps will help you increase your confidence in existing practices and make improvements so that you can start to experience **a significant increase in your customer base**, therefore increasing your revenue.

We've had tremendous success in helping businesses just like yours effectively implement all aspects of our **7-Step Recession-Proofing Process**. We invite you to contact us now at (888) 416-7752 (x101), so you can begin maximizing the revenue potential in your business. Here's the best part: this one-hour business/website analysis consultation is **100% FREE** if you act right away by visiting http://www.lbmsllc.com/marketing-consultation/.

Bottom Line: You need a strong marketing strategy that is centered around your website, which will provide you with a powerful web presence positioning you as an authority in your industry. To do that, your website must convert a high percentage of the visitors into customers. Your website ought to do that for you on autopilot.

If you're not converting about 40 - 50% of your new ideal customers via your website consistently and easily, then your existing marketing strategy isn't strong enough. Not doing so could be putting your business in jeopardy (maybe that's even why you picked up this book). In fact, research shows that if you don't start using innovative and more robust inbound marketing strategies and start using this **7-Step Recession-Proofing Process**, then you could be out of business sooner than you think.

We both know you don't want that to happen, right?

We'd love to hear your implementation stories, too. Share your success stories with us by emailing them to success@lbmsllc.com.

10 RESOURCES

Passion
- Simon Sinek, *What's your Why?*
- Chris Attwood & Janet Bray Attwood, *The Passion Test*

Build Your Brand
- Jonah Berger, *Contagious*

Your Lead Generating Website
- Randy Milanovic, *Building a Better Business Website*

The "No-Brainer" Offer
- Dee Briggs, *5 Steps to Create a Compelling Offer You Can't Refuse*

The Stair-Step Sales Funnel
- Ray Leone, *Success Secrets of the Sales Funnel*

Fortune is in the Follow-Up
- Manny Nowak, *My Sales Follow Up Sucks*

The 4 Rs of Marketing
- Frank Demming,
  Proven Marketing Systems that will Ensure 25% Growth (http://thelocalbusinessguy.com/)

ABOUT THE AUTHOR

Frank Demming (a.k.a. "The Local Business Guy") means business. Small business, that is. He's a marketing expert with a proven track record of helping localized businesses from all over the world increase their revenue by at least 25% within 12 months. His careful analysis of a business's current state results in step-by-step implementation plan paired with careful nurturing. His delighted clients become longtime fans! Frank's a devout New York Yankees fan who lives with his wife in New Jersey.

www.ingramcontent.com/pod-product-compliance
Lightning Source LLC
Chambersburg PA
CBHW041112180526
45172CB00001B/212